The
Rusty Dusty

Childhood for dummies

LUCA CORLATTE

DEDICATION

Dedicated to my daughter Sofia Maria and her mother
Alexandra Tudor.
In memory of my mother Maria and my father Bucur.

Published in October 2022 with the occasion of
Alexandra's most beautiful birthday and Sofia's 9th
celebration a month later.

'La multi ani ani, dragele mele!'

My true home is near these mountains.
Credits: Alexandra Tudor

CONTENTS

Table of Contents

ACKNOWLEDGMENTS

Thanks to my younger self, my effervescent
daughter
and my quirky wife.
Without them my World would not exist.

1

The story of Sunshine the Pekinese dog and his red rusty dusty

You will kindly ask yourself: 'What do dogs and paint have in common?' Hold that thought.

My maternal grandparents had an old corn barn and a Pekinese dog called Sunshine filled with the joys of spring. One lived inside the other, tied to a pole. Barked for affection. Growled for fondness. Howled for friendship. I responded to all these feelings with constant care and attention.

However, I was only visiting my grandparents and experiencing a sentiment of undue care about my surroundings. Honestly, I was a little menace in the baking. Sunshine didn't know about this dark side of mine yet and wasn't suspecting anything either. He was a prisoner of the corn barn simply because people back then found dogs not only dangerous, but in our case, annoying – for being too loving, licking and touching everything. Enough to punish the poor mini-mutt by treating him like an immigrant that didn't manage to jump the border fence (yet). And if that wasn't enough, some corn was shipped the evening before into the barn, almost crushing the mutt which now had to stand in an awkward position. His rusty dusty was facing the fence and getting exposed to (un-friendly) passers-by.

It was a hot summer day, and under a scorching

sun there wasn't much to do for genuine fun. Everything was in a state of advanced ripeness. Like the legendary apple that suffers in silence until that dreadful day when it falls and hits Newton's head. What can you do with time in a day like this? It takes time to save time! A grown-up would completely shut down, pronto. Not me though, I resisted the sleepy space-time continuum that was trying to hack my primary instinct of having fun.

I resorted to my emergency option; my grandad's tools shed. A gizmo in there will satisfy my thirst for knowledge and destruction. I immediately noticed some red paint, lid left open carelessly from a morning paintjob that did not end in time for the afternoon siesta. A few ideas rushed through my mind like a formula one car: painting the apples red so they would be more attractive for the family pig, Goliat; painting some of my hair for a new look – I quickly let that one disperse considering unwanted repercussions at school; painting the headlights of the car for a spooky evening experience; painting a big red cross on the car to make it look like an ambulance; and, finally, painting the small stainless steel bearing balls in red to make them look like tic-tacs – surely these would prove useful later.

The heat was starting to make an impact on me, and whilst I was painting a green apple red, I suddenly hear Sunshine barking in the barn, severely agitated by the same heat. Like a bear in the spring after hibernation, my eyes twinkle at the sight of Sunshine's derrière, clearly visible under his reverse lollipop shaped tail. What if my red paint could decorate the rather appalling looking chocolate starfish?

Bright red, cute round with an exasperating black dot in the middle, a gorgeous work of (red) art. Brighter than Renoir's clown, more subtle than Raphael's churchman and more playful than Monet's Madame Kimono.

Sunshine was screaming like an ambulance. I thought that was the sound of pleasure, how could one (mini mutt) dislike my art (so much). The extreme heat was meddling with my art, peeling it millimetre by millimetre and increasing the suffering tenfold.

To make things even more exciting, grandad shows up, detects Sunshine's predicament, and saves the hurting heinie with fresh gasoline. This makes the poor mutt squeal even louder, saving a terribly boring day from being wasted.

Phew!

2

The story of the sinister plot from under the dinner table

Imagine a huge dinner table, one that can extend allowing for those extra spaces under it where various parts combine. It sat in my living room, right in the centre, leaving a small patch of oriental carpet to guide a trespasser to the balcony. I loved to put myself out of sight under it, concealing my thoughts and intentions, secretly plotting against provoking parents. Obscurity achieved to perfection with the help of a long, dark tablecloth, that allowed just enough light to cram through.

One apparently colourless evening, I suddenly have that funny feeling of imminent carnage. The signs were so obvious, my sixth sense never fails me: low voice dialogues, sizzling sounds of sausage bathed in smelly sunflower oil and an undertone radio sound to complete my conspiracy. Wrongdoing was close to ensue and I was not going to authorise such folly.

I quickly picked up my defenders, a pair of small tacks specifically designed not only to incapacitate trespassers, but to inflict sufficient damage and distress that they will forever lack the courage to attempt an invasion of my territory. Ever again. One tack sat next to a red rose printed on the carpet to camouflage any injury, whilst the other was intelligently placed inside a red lint.

Bam! The first victim yelled their heart out from the excruciating pain, cursed instinctively and retreated in shame. Minutes later, the second tack annihilated another victim in a matter of nanoseconds.

The tacks had accomplished their purpose: to prevent my territory from being invaded by peeving parents and for my balcony to remain under my reign.

Victory was mine yet again!

3

The story of the hidden crown bijou

That wonder for the little priceless things that grown-ups misplace has forever haunted me. And I was not alone! My two pesky cousins were on to it, continually plotting to beat me to the treasure.

There it was, a drawer inside my uncle's barn filled with old mechanical watches, colourful military badges, shiny combs, golden rings, hair pins of all shapes and sizes, ancient pens and crayons some engraved with familiar names, vintage ID size photos depicting funny looking versions of my uncle and aunt, a locket that you could open to find more hilarious photos, small stainless steel balls and lots and lots of buttons engraved with coat of arms.

My attention was drawn to this bijou watch that my aunt surely must have misplaced since it was in a pristine condition, smooth and burnished like I have never seen before. Little old wide-eyed me was amazed!

My wicked cousins were nowhere to be seen, but somehow, I could constantly hear their annoying voices interrogating my bantam life. I grabbed the watch, careful not to leave my marks on it, afraid that in a doomsday scenario, I shall be exposed (by a Poirot look-a-like). I quickly made myself unseen running with Olympian motivation towards my grandparents' house. I did however suspect that a pair or more of snitching eyes have glanced upon my hurried escape!

My grandparent's house had a large industrial gate for an entrance with a small door on the side, a car sized hall continued by a rectangular bare ground loggia. The corners of the quadrangle had pots of lovely petunias and lavender. Vines were delicately providing shade further giving the feeling of a summer veranda, where my grandad would count his egalitarian achievements.

The west side of the quadrangle was gated, but you could easily see farm animals through, mostly the chicken since the pigsty, housing Yin and Yang, was thrown more to the right, behind the house and close to the summer outhouse. Stinky place!

I had this entire maze to my disposal for hiding my newfound treasure. But what could this perfect place be? Where would my pesky cousins never dare nor think to look?

I first thought pigsty, but I wouldn't dare going in there and disturb the Beicon family. Then I thought about the inside of the small barn where we kept Sunshine the Pekinese dog, still recovering after a red paint accident. But no, because they would indeed dare to go in there.

Then it struck me! The pots with petunias! The bijou watch, inside a small protective bag of course, found its ultimate hiding place. Under the petunias!

It felt like that time before a storm when it

does not rain yet, the clouds are bursting with meteorological anger, and you just stand and watch doom unfold. They had arrived, the two Peskies. The not only had seen me earlier, but somehow knew what I had hidden from them. I saw it in their meddling eyes. It was the first time I felt my blood become bubbly like sparkling water almost popping my head off.

They went straight for the usual suspects. And searched and searched for hours and hours. The bijou was nowhere to be found. I sat there watching the special search operation until lightning struck! One of the Peskies found it! Or so he said he did... But my brain was stuck on a fast loop of high delirium, so I rushed straight for the petunias, pulled it up and displayed the bijou to the Peskies proudly, saying:

'See, you didn't find it, because it's right here!'

4

The story of the killer Borner slicer

The colour television with its 25 channels was still considered a miracle. What better way to waste time than watching shows that promise to sell you the solution to every possible household problem.

My mother was polyvalent, she could deliver a proper engineering job, keep the household in order and her favourite son in school – daily. My father had a full 16 hours per day job repairing 'unintellivisions'.

It was a rare occasion pausing the same Centurions episode seen for the 500th time in exchange for my mother's preference. It was revealed to us, a unique slicer in the human world, with maniacal powers, able to squash the toughest and most stubborn tomatoes. German made, Borner, implicitly making it the top successor for the sharpest knife and best cook in existence. Humankind has a long-standing obsession with the sharpness of knives and other deadly cutters. However, most blades are today only made from plastic and handled by four-year-old brats. The German slicer was on a completely different level with four different thicknesses delivering exquisite cubes and *julienne strips*. The description was saying that 'the handy shape makes cutting child's play' – bingo!

People were watching these shows religiously during those post-egalitarian eye-opening times. The show was creating a hypnotic connection with the viewer and their wallet. You are alone in the universe discovering this magical device with nobody else aware of the ground-breaking innovation being expertly tested in front of you (except the expert). The price offer seemed equally unbelievable, but not to me. It was costing more than my arm and my leg.

However, my savings didn't have to contribute so I happily *cheerleadered* from the side-lines. A few days passed by and finally, we saw the contraption in front of us. Shiny, smooth, lustrous and a wee scary because of its razor-sharp ninja blades.

I swiftly observe my mother decipher its uses, think that I'm on to it and have a go myself. Waldorf salad with sliced apples… and a thin cut index finger slice! I was looking into the bowl terrified and amazed at the same time. A chunk of my *digitus secundus* was bathing harmoniously in the apple and lemon juice.

The rest of the finger seemed right out of a biology lesson studying dissection.

I quickly took my bloody body part out before I could get sick from the sight of it, mummified my finger with extra soft premium toilet paper and shipped the salad as a good neighbour gesture to the lovely family living at floor one.

Bone appétit!

5

The story of the Continents versus Tomato Kid

My mother was super proud of me during my pre-adolescence years. Like any responsible parent, she wanted to show off to others what an unbelievably smart progeny she has unleashed into the egalitarian world.

Every child has some sort of admiration for the globe. It looks like a strange ball that you can kick. But then, you realise that it's a lamp. And finally, you are told (by a grown-up) that you are located right there on the globe under the pointer. Obviously, you would then think that with a microscope, you will be able to see a much smaller version of yourself. I tried this, could not find myself and then started crying thinking that I died!

After my sixth birthday, I learned how to appreciate and respect the globe. It was so colourful with beautiful bright bluish tones, with atmospheric features, primarily its whirling white cloud decorations and frozen white poles. These were opposed by the dark blue of the oceans. Expanding dark-gold deserts over the lifeful green Edens where hobbits hang out. The oceans are truly enigmatic with their unexplored depths, whereas the continents are so gripping that I kept rotating my globe hundreds of times hoping that new worlds appear with every turn.

The ultimate realisation for me was to learn the continents. I had managed to do so before I was six. A fact which, evidently, my mother so much desired to exploit. And so, one fateful day, my older than me niece – yes, I inexplicably have an older niece – was visiting us as per usual manner. She was talking to my mother about how her hand disappears when she places it between her eyes. As the miracle of the invisible hand was being demystified, I was most affectionately asked to recite the continents.

I could never concentrate enough to be able to demonstrate my true talents. This was one of those moments. I tried to say Arctic first thinking that because it's a frozen ocean, it would dissipate my body's usual reaction to pressure and turn into a shy tomato. No such luck, I was the split image of the fruit-vegetable. Seeing me struggle, my mother had a whip-smart idea. I could recite from under the kitchen table where all the shy children hang about. Delighted with this unexpected solution to my livid crimson predicament, I jumped down under the kitchen table in order to discharge my talent: 'Arctic, North Atlantic, South Atlantic, North Pacific, South Pacific, Indian, and Southern oceans.'

My niece clapped enthusiastically, lifted the tablecloth, only to find Tomato Kid under it!

6

The story of the super awkward bath

A hot summer day on a weekend meant a bubble bath was in order. I had the same admiration for bathtubs as the Romans did. For them, baths were an object of mutiny, revolt, love and worship (of the goddess Sulis Minerva). For me... I felt like a selfish giant in my personal *mediterrana* and absolutely nothing could change my heart.

Elsewhere in our insipid cuboid of concrete, my father was plotting with a handy man about herculean changes to be made to our kitchen and balcony, linking them together for eternity and making redundant my tack infested access prevention system in the living room.

I could easily hear their voices trying to figure out some minor final details and, eventually, exchanging the usual pleasantries that are said at the end of a conversation. Especially by my self-righteous father. He repeats the same polite words in a hallucinating manner to overwhelm his victims. Alas, silence at last!

All seemed dandy and splendiferous as I was admiring my wrinkled fingertips submerged in bath water and rehearsing my playing dead in the bathtub routine (freaking my mother out every single time). Suddenly, the bathroom door shrieks open. Looking at me straight in the eye was the handy man, visibly disturbed by what he was about to do. I hear my father's voice in the background asking me not to mind as the immoral foreigner had an exceptional emergency to deal with. This was one of the most disturbing group of seconds in my whole life. Comparable only to flatulating in a crowded lift or realising that your pants are down in front of older respectable people or your love crush.

The first second took the longest. It started with a blink in his right eye followed by a swift observation of the toilet set-up with his other eye so he could install himself and spend a penny in it. The second second was terrifying. It involved his pants being pulled down from the back such that his *johnson* stays covert. This second was followed by three more seconds of whooshing noises and a fourth bearing the sounds of a *micro-fartie* mixed with a droplet of grown-up weewee (disgusting!). Seconds one and two, he stared at me with the eyes of a disturbing cat, to which I responded with impeccable hostility. The last second he grinned at me senselessly, his perverted way of saying thank you to a naked child. What a blithering idiot!

Did I mention that I was naked? Completely naked. With a man in his 40s having a quick wee in a 40 square foot bathroom whilst I was taking a bath? In   my   bathroom?!   Mamma   mia!

7

The story of Captain Pharmacist

Why move people from the open free countryside to the gloomy cities? It makes no sense at all. But this was my pre-adolescence fate, to live inside and within insipid cuboids of concrete. All the kids were allowed outside time, hours and hours of wasted youth performing the most idiotic deeds instead of memorising egalitarian propaganda or rehearsing the quadratic formula.

I was minding my own business skipping thoughts when I suddenly hear shouting in my direction.

All of you block 43 (i.e. insipid cuboid) kids go away, we block 45 kids have unanimously decided that you are trespassing our territory, playing our games, misusing our toys, touching our pets! No more!

Being outnumbered, I swiftly relented and was on my way to home base when a Samaritan voice rescued me. He is OK, but the others must go, especially Horseface.

To ratify my membership to the select club, we have started throwing pieces of chalk against the 20-meter side-wall of block 42, carefully avoiding the little bathroom windows that were puncturing it, looking like cave houses from Cappadocia. Football followed on the dusty surface in front of block 43,

irresponsibly ignoring efforts made by our neighbour, Captain Pharmacist, to turn our little corner of hell into a green land of milk and honey. He made his appearance, being visibly disturbed and frustrated, yelling with one jaw in the sky and the other on the ground that he will see us severely punished for our insensitivity towards Mother Nature. Nobody but the Pharmacist wanted to save the Planet back then, he was our unwanted and unrecognised planetarian superhero.

He noticed me especially, probably because of how my yet undiscovered respect for his planet saving efforts was betrayed by my guilty looks. We each retreated to our home base calling it the day. Cursing silently, he disappeared to his 2nd floor observation point. That's that I thought. Much to my amazement, he showed up at our door explaining to my father all the incriminating events in perfect chronological order, Poirot style.

Minutes later, my father returned to my room, smiling and asking sarcastically if I agree to having my bottom clapped, since this was a direct request from Captain Pharmacist. My views about physical violence accorded well with my father's so there will be no bottom clapping tonight.

Captain Pharmacist awayyy!

8

The story of the stubborn sticky paint

I was in a love relationship with paint from a very young age – my first love. The way it flows, spews and spills, but most importantly, the way it sticks to things. Children will forever in the history of humankind have a particular fascination with paint and its descendants: goo, sludge, ooze, gunk and my personal favourite, slime.

I was in my salad days during those prehistoric egalitarian times. We happened to have a large pot of white paint available for various household improvements and repairs. With this occasion, there was extra paint available due to what can only be described as a construction site in my kitchen. My father was aiming to connect the kitchen to the balcony by deliberately hammering a reinforced 45-centimetre-thick wall. The noise he was making entered the skulls of every single living being in a 1-kilometre radius and was surely producing some irreversible effects. I clearly remember one neighbour behaving very strangely after the deed was done – he fed his 3-year-old goldfish to his ragdoll cat which he then punished by taking it to a barber friend to trim and made it look like a French poodle. So, a Poodle Cat. Yuck!

Having observed the paint for some time, I wasn't going to allow for it to simply dry on a wall. It had to be thoroughly inspected by my still under development talents. Both parents were away to cut a Gordian knot. I seized the moment, approached the gooey substance, and submerged my right hand in it completely, no questions asked. I was dumbstruck by a group of feelings normally associated with winning a gold medal at the Olympics, jubilation and triumph mixed with perfect and pure white mass (of gunge).

The experiment went on for a good while. I must congratulate myself for instinctively not compromising my left hand with the inedible whipping cream. Time to get it off, my right hand goes under the water tap only for me to realise that small bubbles were appearing and disappearing in a magical loop on top of the gunge. It was probably my first real encounter with panic. Being more sensitive than your (un)usual brat, I unleashed a storm of tears doubled by a continuum of vocals.

My distress was identified by a peeping neighbour, an older than me girl that jumped to the rescue. You would think that rescuers empathise with their victims, especially small children. Not in this peculiar case. Her facial expressions were hitting clear notes of 'look at stupid'. She then grabbed my mother's nail polish remover, poured all of it on my glowing hand, and magic!

My mother arrived home later only to turn the initial smile into a grin and criticise her tormented offspring for wasting her remover.

Bah humbug!

9

The story of Echo from under the birthday party table

I was obligated to attend social events. Every molecule in my body, every atom sized morsel was opposing the useless bonding between young whippersnappers. One neighbour was acting as the leader of the party pack. There is always one Dionysus per square mile. Ready with mountains of cuisine, vol-au-vents, cheese-puffs, salads, pastas and tarts, tenderloins and fuzzy liquids, cookies arranged in tactical soldier formations and eclipsed by a humongous cake darted with numbered candles. Flanked by some quick cheats for the elders. This bit was OK.

It was now celebration time and, unfortunately, I was invited. The OK bit had consumed with the speed of candlelight, and we were all now entering bonding territory. The music was getting gradually louder and even my thoughts needed to be shouted. I was practically, tactically and strategically avoiding to immerse myself into the madness unfolding in front of me. Thankfully, there was nothing particularly interesting about me, which meant that my attempts to hide in plain sight were pretty successful. Only the occasional *hi-hellos* accompanied by grins from ear to ear and, rarely, by stressful hugs and cheek kisses.

An unexpected technology advancement at this jamboree was the introduction of a video camera. My hiding tactics were going to become a video c(o)urse. I did not even notice music, when mixed with my get-away-as-quickly-as-possible thoughts, it changed frequency to a tone that only Echo could conceive.

But Echo then took human form and asked me to dance! The horror! I was found and exposed! Despite the harshness of my rejection, Echo's attempts to drag me into ignominy only amplified. Desperate for a way out and knowing that I cannot leave the room, I found respite in the only shaded place in the room, under the party table. Echo swiftly pointed to the wolf pack that I was attempting to elude. What I can only describe as mean and irresponsible, the grown-up manning the video camera, flashed it inside my newly discovered escape route.

I was a shy, solitude loving Narcissus, finding refuge under the world. If you think my plan B

worked, you are so wrong. It failed miserably and Echo pulled me out, we danced (read random illogical movement of legs and arms) whilst the excitement around my failed prison break was slowly fading away. Echo then whispered to me: 'Oh marvellous boy, I loved you in vain, farewell'. She was gone to torture someone else.

Alas poor Narcissus – the real one – he kicked the bucket!

10

The story of Grandad's elder thorns

Old people are thoroughly strange. I think they know they are. They also do it on purpose to appear crazy or just about and thus expect humble understanding and free service all the time. A negligible small proportion don't do it on purpose of course, they are simple, lovely and helpless dying old people. This yarn concerns my grandad on my mother's side, long standing medalled comrade during the regime with an assumed masculine authority the size of Jupiter.

Nonetheless, even these overachieving titans fear of becoming old and helpless. Grandchildren can prove very handy in these awkward situations, they can scratch the un-scratchable, massage the un-massageable, feed the un-feedable. The little ones can also be visually threatened by the old geriatrics, unlike their parents.

It was a beautiful summer day with my grandad stuck with me, alone in the insipid cuboid. I was minding my own business, quasi-faking a homework and watching Galtar and the Golden Lance and how he was defeating Tormack the tyrant for the 500th time. Grandad kept interrupting my breathing space with boring memories from his millennial past. Still, I must appreciate him for leaving shortly after each recollection and not sticking by for feedback. For his last disturbance of the day, he had no more memories to galvanise me into pure boredom. Instead, he unkindly and rather domineeringly ordered me to trim his ear hairs with my favourite pair of scissors. How despicable is that?

He had this satisfied look of a man about to eat a fresh marmalade sandwich. I had the look of a Frizzle chicken before being butchered. Inexplicably, I relented to the horrid task and carefully identified candidate follicles. Soon, I determined that he wasn't going to be able to inspect my work. Thus, I decided to cut his elder thorns at different lengths just for fun. Bad idea, the old barn still had hands to use and managed to uncover my covert operation.

That's when he asked me if I could use my mother's wax station instead.
How despicable is that?

11

The story of the offended farm lady

I simply adore travelling – but much more the getting there. By train, by coach and less by plane (or rockets). On this occasion, I was finally travelling alone, undisturbed, on a coach that was heading from west to south crossing a vast plain followed by pair of foggy mountains. My place on a backseat of the coach was remarkably comfortable. No seat neighbour and a huge window providing me with high resolution views of people and places.

With the view becoming more and more jerky

because of the increasing speed of the coach and the radio music inside the coach becoming less and less noticing, I soon received a call from Slumber Land. That felling lasted for exactly three seconds because my stomach made an unexpected statement. It growled, then it rumbled and finally it gurgled. I was in shock, witnessing this barbarity. Wishful thinking that this was only a temporary disturbance in the force. It was not. The sounds amplified, changed length, volume, and frequency, enough to make myself heard by fellow travellers.

I did what I thought most people do – I

sucked it in. I tried a soft massage too, literally tickling myself in the hope to fool the unstable breadbasket. No chance in heaven because events soon became neurotic. The despicable goo wanted to make contact with open air. Only, I was in a coach!

Rarely and randomly, life demands you to make split-second decisions. I jumped straight up, almost teleported myself to the driver to whom I whispered heavily: 'Either you stop the coach right now, or I give you a sample of Montezuma's revenge right here!'. We were mid-way between towns with a flurry of houses visible. I descended the coach being closely inspected by fellow travellers, feeling their frustration developing.

Next to the road, thankfully, there was a peasant dwelling place. Strangely enough, it did not benefit from any fences, easily allowing me to radar scan for a natural lavatory. Identified! A cavity in the ground decorated by sweepings and junk. I immediately entered flash discard mode. In my lightning plunge, I had forgotten my reusable baby wipes in the coach. But I noticed a piece of paper that destiny placed there for me, the Thought, a respectable newspaper.

Whist reaching for the newspaper, I hear a shouted voice from not afar. It was the owner of the place, visibly offended by my intrusion and asking why I didn't use the human lavatory, proudly standing five meters away from me. I photo finish my fertilisation event, swipe the Thought and whizz back to the coach under heavy surveillance by the offended farm lady, her stupid dog, the merciful driver, her sleeping assistant and 39 other frustrated fellow travellers.

Shamefaced like never again!

12

The story of tick box bread

Pre-adolescence life was fantastic. I could explore everything non-stop. Trouble began when my exploration included grown-up stuff such as syringes, medication, funny looking balloons, paint and important documents. Making a mess of my father's blood flow injections translated into six double bottom claps. Eating a whole box of Vitamin D chewies guaranteed a trip to the hospital to check for effects and side effects.

A piece of paper had puzzled me intensely. It had 31 small, numbered boxes on it, with a few of those consecutively marked with an X. It appeared to resemble a multi-row biathlon target. The paper was scribbled daily, religiously, a routine that only bureaucratic grown-ups can concoct. One day, I decided to shoot my own 'X' on it to see what happens next and if I could break the annoying routine.

Surprisingly, that same day, my mother became stuck between chores and was obligated to deputy me for the most important task that I was ever given. I was provided with real money, the piece of paper that I had marked moments earlier and was sent to buy three breads. It was a historical moment for me to be entrusted with such a critical goal. Feeding the family of three depended on my juvenile ability to deliver!

The bread store was moments away. I patiently waited in the queue for about 45 minutes, proudly flashing the tick box card to announce my new *status quo*. Mrs Bread Lady looked terrifying; I had always suspected that she ate small children when her shop was out of bread. She asked for the tick box card and grabbed two breads which she then catapulted into my bread bag.

I could not understand why one bread was missing, she swiftly explained with a roar that one of the tick boxes is ticked, thus the 3rd bread was to be withdrawn. This outcome resulted into a river of cry that could impress the best Hollywood film director. A few susceptible grown-ups reacted to my spasms of hurt and summoned goddess Clementia to intervene.

To my surprise, Mrs Bread Lady relented and awarded me with the missing bread. I rushed home only to be told that we have infinite freedom from today and that the dictator had fled in a helicopter.

But I had been free for my entire life, so what was changing for me?

13

The story of the disappeared Buddha

It was a special evening visiting our close relatives. There was chitter-chatter between the grown-ups and some tittle-tattle for the children. It was that time when the sun goes to have his beauty sleep and the golden light protected by the Atlantides, the evening daughters of Night, survives for another hour. Magical events take place during this hour, one can see, if lucky, light pillars and sundogs until the sun goes 6 degrees below the horizon.

Because of the increased sensitivity of the information that I was carefully sharing with my nieces and little nephew, the conversation was taking place under the extended dinner table. In combination with the golden hour, the effect it had on me can only be compared with munching my mother's choux à la crème, a delicatesse unparalleled in deliciousness by any other mortal cook.

Close to the table was a free-standing shelf that had the most astonishing Buddha mini-statuette right in the middle, giving the whole construct the feel of a centuries old mausoleum. At a point, I stopped listening to any of the yackety-yak around me and concentrated on the statuette and its sensational golden crust.

Dinner was being served and the absence of witnesses meant that I could finally position myself closer and touch the statuette, allowing its superpowers to pass on to me. Once in my hands, the bond was hypnotical, similar to the one between identical twins. The thought of not being able to hold it for longer shortly became an obsession. It had to be mine! No villainous laughs followed though; I was laser focused.

I hid it deep inside my clothes, to the point where it was making skin contact and making me laugh. I kept my composure with an aura of invincibility, whilst Buddha was shielding me from any foe. Arriving home with the avatar, my parents receive a phone call. A familiar voice claims the disappearance of the golden statuette. I had been discovered and whilst wholly ashamed of my deed, Buddha was looking straight at me and providing me with the solace that I so desperately needed.

I visited Buddha every Sunday for the next few months at my relative's shrine. No surprise that by the end of my godly addiction, I had managed to 'resolutely train myself to attain peace'!

14

The story of the missing capital

Frogg lived at the first floor of our insipid cuboid of concrete. He had a large family compared to mine which meant that he had fewer material possessions, but many more emotional. His parents both had odious ways of dealing with the cruelty of life in the city. Despite these flaws in the fabric of his childhood, Frogg had an adorable guilty smile as his default facial expression. He was indeed a little rascal, but his pranks and stunts were sincere and ingenuous.

School season has started for a few weeks,

and I was moderately submerged into lessons and homework – you could call this the Herculean learning style. It is probably not a coincidence that Hercules had twelve labours to endure, the same number of years one was expected to absorb high calorie knowledge. I was not going to be a demi-god, but I could not let Cerberus defeat me either.

One evening around Pi Day, after taking the garbage out to the usual place in the unsanitary centre of our egalitarian rectangle of cuboids, my mother returns home with Frogg. He was going to receive a taste of maths and calligraphy writing under the supervision of me and my mother.

We start writing a few sentences about our worst fears. I write about poo on a stick, a villainous practice that has one running for his life. Frogg wrote about an event in the past centred around his father's cast of mind. Then I realised that he had his father's name written with a lower-case letter. Immediately, my mother corrected him whilst he was displaying his usual guilty smile. He then makes the same mistake again, mis-writing the same name.

The lessons ended with Frogg unconvincingly leaving towards his home. I later went to sleep after the loud quarrelling sounds from the cuboid below silenced and thinking that I had also learned a lesson today.

One should go against the grain when treated unfairly!

15

The story about the centre of my galaxy

Being small and helpless, I was not allowed to leave the egalitarian rectangle of cuboids alone. A guardrail of my early existence never to explore beyond. Usually, as a child, you are confined to a place resembling heaven and thus protected from the unpredictable and savage outside world. In my case, the situation was more in reverse. It felt like living on an insignificant and inescapable planet inside a galaxy that was rich, vast and massive.

I soon began dreaming about visiting other parts of my galaxy. I actually visited a couple of times, only for my dream to end with my father popping my bubble with his melodramatic morning tune *'Mister Getupson!'*. As much as Morpheus allowed me to see it, the centre of my galaxy was bright and twinkling, decorated with many banners and lights. The shops were colourful and filled with alien thingamajigs and thingamabobs that I could barely control myself to touch. This special shop right in the centre had the name of a mountain and it was layered on many levels with each dedicated to specific types of visitors – like Starship Enterprise!

Not only that I dared to break the guardrails one day, but I also managed to secure a significant amount of blue bank notes. I did not do it alone, my trusty older-than-me niece served her role of cicerone. I felt that I could not walk in the same way outside my guardrails as I do within, so I brought with me my special shoes with bubbles and the most inconspicuous steel grey clothes. We were now way outside of my safety isle and slowly approaching the target – a toy shop called Toy Brains that was selling the most spectacular collection of toy cars.

I spent the whole amount available, seized the goods and speed walked slightly faster than the local bus towards home. I was happy and scared at the same time – a strange feeling that, later I found out, was called *anxiety* or how to be responsible for your own happiness.

Face to face with the reaction of my father when he found out about my mischievous plan and, most importantly, that I had executed it. I received a recognition of my merits in the form of four bottom claps (easy!), 60 decibels worth of warning for just under 8 seconds and my cash account frozen indefinitely. In all the commotion, I managed to keep the Bavarian cars collection, R2-D2 and a high-quality set of brain prints about life in the rest of the galaxy.

The centre of my galaxy, the final frontier. These were the voyages of a little shy boy. '*His five-year old* mission: to explore strange new worlds, to seek out new life and new civilisations, to boldly go where no   *miniature-man*   has   gone   before!'

16

The story of Neighbour Measles

There were more and more days lately that I would find myself alone at home. Power and freedom! I wouldn't have trusted myself alone in a home with gas and electricity, not to mention paint and other gooey stuff. Any random event that could occur such as a neighbour knocking and asking for a flash-loan or putting off a fire in the kitchen, I would be there, entrusted by elders to protect the land.

It was three-bad-hours Tuesday and normally I should have been at school by now. Instead, I had exposed myself unwillingly to a virus – the measles –

and it brought with it a suite of bodily manifestations of the most despicable form. My sneezing would have

 broken the speed limit on any highway, my nose worked as badly as an old tap, my body benefited from additional heating and finally, the most peculiar red spots, all over my body, making me look like I was just attacked by a

battalion of flies – all at the same time – with the ceremonial itchiness. Heavenly rest is all you want to do and it makes all the sense in the world – my body was sending vast armies to fight this invader.

Just after lunch, I hear the doorbell chiming. I knew from the elders that on Tuesdays, even the smallest problems can easily become twisted and complicated – Mars the god of War would see to it himself. My lovely neighbour Bob(escu), living diagonally on the same floor, was unusually curious about my condition. I did not open the door to protect him. Because I was that kind of person of course. Plus, I had to avoid triggering the three-bad-hours. However, he continued to ask me questions, including a huge favour. He allegedly had never seen the red spots before and since I was in what seemed to be the last day having to fight the virus, could I not allow him to see the repugnant spots for a split second. I relented because I was that kind of person of course. To my little surprise, the door was widely pushed open, Bob(escu) ushered himself inside and started taking deep breaths of infected air particles.

Despite his nonsensical attempt, the virus was not interested in him as a host, or was immediately annihilated, which is a strong possibility given his obsession with garlic (his uncle's name was Vlad). Bob(escu) still had to go to school and do chores until spring school holiday season saved his soul.

Next year, he had the measles too, during Christmas break. He was desperate Santa would not visit him that year to avoid infection, so he put my address on Santa's letter. Thank you, Santa!

17

The story of Pencil Box boy

School was a strict place and teachers had the option to literally act like our parents should the situation require it. This did not include bottom clapping, however did include a softer version of pre-human-rights times child punishment practices. I managed to avoid such an event with complete success. It would have been impossible to find me as the cause (or even root cause) of any of the non-compliant activities regularly occurring in my class.

Several behaviours, habits and exploits that I had concocted were keeping the purple cane away from my hands. One of these practices was my stylish, perfectly organised pencil box. I was able to pimp my pencil box with elegance, finesse and, most importantly, geometrical precision. Handmade and improvised stickers usually extracted from my mother's collection of *Neckermann* magazines, small extra pockets housing miniature gizmos and contraptions, the usuals in various sizes and shapes and, most importantly, my pen. A *Jinhao* fountain pen with Chinese origins stood proudly in the dedicated section of the pencil box. My pen licence arrived relatively early thanks to that pen. I was systematically making sure that it is full of blue ink – a feeling that I experienced again years later, charging my phone immediately as the charge went below 80%.

My fellow colleagues were intrigued about my pencil box. One day, a few of the top girls in the class asked me if they could take a closer look. Admiration, jealousy, praise and wonder, all directed at me and my pencil box. My fountain pen was also thoroughly inspected. The lesson started and I began writing when I realised that my pen was not printing the ink properly on the paper. It was clear soon that it wasn't my pen, so I looked around to find that the girl in front of me, Floweret, was writing with an identical pen. I quickly accused the terrible event, only to be told by the teacher that I have no evidence of the pens getting mixed up. Being a descendent of great warriors including the Dacians and the Romans, I started crying due to the injustice that I was a victim of. It is worth noting that my reputation of a crier started on that day and that it took me gargantuan efforts until years later to shake it off.

Frustration time! Arriving home, my mother acknowledged the dreadful mix and talked to the teacher the next day. This resulted in absolutely nothing.

Will not Thoth, the god of learning and writing, avenge me?!

18

The story about unprecedented unthinkable events

Shyness was an emotion that I was exceedingly good at. I displayed it continuously, when speaking and when not speaking. I only stopped in my sleep, my dreams were about unusual heroes and explosions (of thermal power stations predominantly) that the heroes could not prevent. I was changing colour several times a day, accompanied by heavy sweating due to my supernatural sudiferous glands. I was in perfect antithesis with a poker face, probably a reason why playing card games never appealed to me.

Surprisingly, this uncomfortable superpower did have advantages too. I was excluded from events that could embarrass me such as those involving dancing or speaking to an audience. But most importantly, people seemed to trust me more – and I never betrayed their trust. Mostly because I literally could not. It also involved a certain level of reliability that others could extract from me. I was a safe bet.

One late Friday at school, I managed to surpass all my previous records in embarrassment. During my previous to last class, my stomach started making sounds that, if amplified enough, would terrify even the glamorous Cruella de Vil. Sensing the danger that was about to ensue, I begin applying some highly ineffective stomach sucking techniques. 39 seconds later, my internal alarm systems go off as if I was a nuclear power station. I was about to do the unthinkable: excuse myself to go to the lavatory. Arriving to my unusual destination, which I never before visited, a collection of feelings synonymous with extreme nervousness and panic led me back towards the classroom, achieving a colossal nothing. The horrifying torment continued until break time when the god of all unthinkable events occurred. I filled my underwear with fresh poo. Whilst standing. Properly solid (yay!).

It was fantastic to feel great relief, monumental fear and acute embarrassment, all at the same time. I then broke my panic record again. A few colleagues asked me if I want to play with them, I followed them as if under a spell, disbelieving my condition. Only to stop after a few steps and claim an unbearable abdominal pain. Milliseconds later, I finally understood my predicament and under the extra motivation of a quickly developing odour, I fetched my belongings and rushed home with careful strides, skipping the last class. Again unprecedented.

It was a lesson well learnt, at school, on a Friday!

19

The story about my first curse

Keeping a brat in check is a difficult task. I will always be grateful for my mother for never going beyond bottom clapping with my punishments. Her way of doing it was careful and meticulous, so much so that at some point in my early teenager career, I swapped crying with laughing whilst receiving the claps. But I knew from fellow brats that things could get very complicated and rather dangerous with other parents. Luckily, this was not my case and I learned to appreciate my mother for loving me in the way she did. The clapping stopped eventually and was replaced by reason and well measured argumentation.

I liked to push her limits sensing her weakness towards me. One of my favourites was to mess with her hair. Especially in the family car, a 35 horsepower Dacian monster, when she sat in the passenger seat with me occupying the backseat. Only now I see the other reason for kids wearing seatbelts on the backseats. Sometimes, my answers to her legitimate questions were intentionally imprecise or incomplete, adding to her huge tank of frustration that seemed to take ages to overflow.

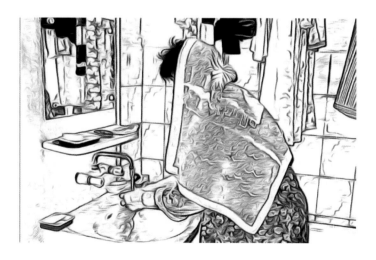

There was an official assumption that spending time in my room would imply making progress with homework. That wasn't really the case, especially with my 160 MHz Pentium supercomputer in the room. Homework was getting harder and more extensive, and this was in direct collision with my newly found information technology interests. Technology can have a toxic effect on a young whippersnapper's ability to control overconfidence and temper. Having been asked to stop wasting time on the computer, my buffer suddenly overflows and I utter words to my mother that can only be qualified as impertinent and disrespectful. Literally, I unkindly asked her to go and visit Hades on her next holiday. She looked into my eyes without making any sound for exactly two seconds and left the room. Those were the longest two seconds I have ever lived and I felt shame dripping over my face like strawberry jam (from Tismana Monastery – yummy!). So much was said without any words being emitted.

With my mother's invisible firewall in place, I have never repeated that exploit ever again.

Acta non verba!

20

The story about the sky shutting down

A starry sky, heavenly mix of mythological glitter. The one good thing about my insipid cuboid is that it had a balcony. The balcony was my territory and there were times when you could only reach it only by going through my specially designed discovery tunnel. The tunnel was decorated with large pillows and small cushions on the sides of set twin chairs facing each other. Moments after the golden hour had ended, I usually found myself admiring the night sky. I wasn't able to benefit from a telescope until much later, but instead I had received a pair of stylish theatre binoculars that made the moon look just slightly larger.

Elders were once saying that the sky is held up by four main stars. I imagined the night sky to be some sort of obscure tablecloth that is slowly laid upon and then taken off us every day, the stars being those minuscule particles of light that managed to slide through the imperfect material. Nobody would be crazy enough to hold it for some many hours, so in theory the myth made sense. The elders also claimed the Moon to be the wife of the Sun. That did not make a lot of sense, unless they had an argument and were now upset.

It was Anno Domini 1999 and my World was preparing for a huge astronomical event. The sky was going to go black completely for a few minutes during the day! I found that most intriguing and was prepared to welcome the event from the top of my cuboid. I was extremely curious to see if werewolves were indeed going to swallow the Moon and the Sun whilst they are distracted. That didn't happen, but what did happen was a mythical increase in sounds made mostly by animals. To them, this event had an ancient significance. We people have altered that to a point where we simply turn the lights on during an eclipse and continue with our routine, laughing in the face of our elders.

There was one notable exception! Having been inspired from a true Columbus story, three days earlier, I asked a pipsqueak to return the sweets that he nabbed from my shopping bag the other day whilst I was reflecting on my inner self. Should he not comply with my demand for restitution, I will summon a werewolf to kidnap him. He will know this because the sky will shut down, lights will turn off, whilst the werewolf is looking for him.

He showed up petrified, all yellow faced, with a bag filled with unhealthy sweets, asking for immediate forgiveness. I hesitantly accepted and asked the sun to return to its rightful place in the sky and scare off the nasty werewolf.

Too bad solar eclipses are so rare, but imagine the possibilities with a lunar eclipse!

About the author

I love this painting. That is all you need to know about me.

Credits: Alexandra Tudor

Back soon…!

Printed in Great Britain
by Amazon

87415290R00049